We All Like It!

Mary Elizabeth Salzmann

Consulting Editor Monica Marx, M.A./Reading Specialist

Published by SandCastle™, an imprint of ABDO Publishing Company, 4940 Viking Drive,
Edina, Minnesota 55435.

Printed in the United States.

Credits
Edited by: Pam Price
Curriculum Coordinator: Nancy Tuminelly
Cover and Interior Design and Production: Mighty Media
Photo Credits: BananaStock Ltd., Comstock, Corbis Images, Digital Vision, Eyewire Images,
ImageState, PhotoDisc, Rubberball Productions

Library of Congress Cataloging-in-Publication Data

Salzmann, Mary Elizabeth, 1968-
     We all like it! / Mary Elizabeth Salzmann.
          p. cm. -- (Sight words)
     Includes index.
     Summary: Uses simple sentences, photographs, and a brief story to introduce six
different words: all, it, like, little, my, see.
     ISBN 1-59197-467-4
     1. Readers (Primary) 2. Vocabulary--Juvenile literature. [1. Reading.] I. Title. II. Series.

PE1119.S23467 2003
428.1--dc21

2003050319

SandCastle™ books are created by a professional team of educators, reading specialists, and
content developers around five essential components that include phonemic awareness,
phonics, vocabulary, text comprehension, and fluency. All books are written, reviewed, and
leveled for guided reading, early intervention reading, and Accelerated Reader® programs
and designed for use in shared, guided, and independent reading and writing activities to
support a balanced approach to literacy instruction.

Let Us Know

After reading the book, SandCastle would like you to tell us your
stories about reading. What is your favorite page? Was there something
hard that you needed help with? Share the ups and downs of learning
to read. We want to hear from you! To get posted on the ABDO
Publishing Company Web site, send us e-mail at:

sandcastle@abdopub.com

SandCastle Level: Beginning

Featured Sight Words

all   it

like   little

my   see

The Smiths all ride on the merry-go-round.

It is a good day for a family picture.

The Webers like to play games.

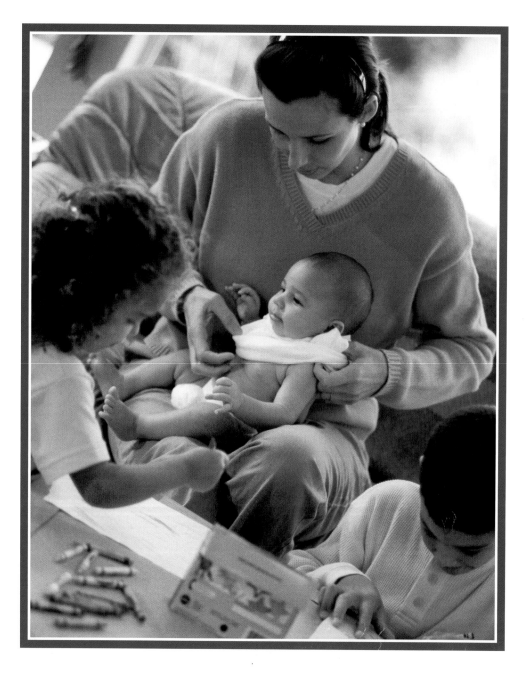

little

Grace and Mark have a little baby brother.

I run on the beach
with my family.

The Kents use
binoculars to
see birds.

Family Swim

My parents and my little brother are my family.

My brother's name is Neal.

Neal is learning how to swim.

See him float in the water.

Mom and Dad
take us swimming
every day.

We all like it at
the pool!

More Sight Words in This Book

a	have	take
and	him	the
are	how	to
at	I	us
day	in	we
for	is	with
good	on	

All words identified as sight words in this book are from Edward Bernard Fry's "First Hundred Instant Sight Words."

Picture Index

baby, p. 11

beach, p. 13

binoculars, p. 15

birds, p. 15

picture, p. 7

pool, p. 20

About SandCastle™

A professional team of educators, reading specialists, and content developers created the SandCastle™ series to support young readers as they develop reading skills and strategies and increase their general knowledge. The SandCastle™ series has four levels that correspond to early literacy development in young children. The levels are provided to help teachers and parents select the appropriate books for young readers.

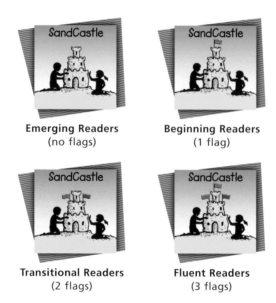

Emerging Readers
(no flags)

Beginning Readers
(1 flag)

Transitional Readers
(2 flags)

Fluent Readers
(3 flags)

These levels are meant only as a guide. All levels are subject to change.

To see a complete list of SandCastle™ books and other nonfiction titles from ABDO Publishing Company, visit www.abdopub.com or contact us at:

4940 Viking Drive, Edina, Minnesota 55435 • 1-800-800-1312 • fax: 1-952-831-1632